The Shortest Book on Dividend Investing

The Shortest Book on Dividend Investing...

By Josh D.

Table of contents

The Basic
3-5

Covid And The Book Worm
5-6

Fees Kill Wealth
7-8

The Rule Of 72
9-10

The World Has Its Hair On Fire
11-13

The Me Tax
14-15

Now What?
16-19

What's In Your Pocket?
20-21

Crypto
21

Who Do You Trust With Your Money
21-23

The basic:

Dividend investing… what is it? First, let's look at the definition of a dividend. A dividend is a sum of money paid regularly by a company to its shareholders out of its profits. Therefore, when you invest some money into a company that pays dividends you get paid more money, and if you reinvest that money, you get more money and more shares which therefore makes you got it… more money. It's money making more money.

Now a chart to show you how much you need to invest to get $100 a year and then $1,000

Ex.

Ticker	Yield	How much to invest to get $100 X=yield/100 $100/x	How much to invest to get $1,000
T	5.91%	$100/.0591= $1,692 invested	$1,000/.0591= $16,920 invested

I always start at $100, why? I know I have to crawl before I can run, etc. I do the above calculation with every stock and index fund I invest in.

All my investing accounts have a DRIP (dividend reinvestment plan). Everything I get paid goes back into the stocks with the ultimate goal being to stop the drip. I look at dividends as little pebbles. Much like the fable of the crow and the pitcher, I use my circumstance to create innovation. The jar being wealth and the water at the bottom is the money I want. Every little pebble or dividend payment brings the water all that closer to the top so I can one day sip it.

The way I look at dividend investing and buying an asset is each dollar is at work it's in a factory 24/7 a robot building more robots.

KO pays $0.44 per share and trades at $63.64 with a dividend yield of 2.74% to get 1 share a year you need to invest $2,323. Invest and hold and boom eventually you will be getting extra shares and some fractional shares to build wealth.

I am kinda lazy, so I just want my asset to sit there and to bluntly put it crap out dividends until it can build more full copies of itself.

COVID and the book worm:

In late 2021 I got sick like almost dead sick. I was in the hospital for a few months and was home for close to 6 to recover. I spent that time reading books and rereading books on investing. I read books like The intelligent investor, Rich Dad Poor Dad, A Random Walk Down Wall Street, The Richest Man in Babylon, and The Little Red Book of Common-Sense Investing. My mind was swirling but it all said the same thing, a recurring theme that really changed my approach.

I wanted to build wealth and I knew it wasn't going to be a quick fly-by-night thing. So, I put the lessons down on paper.

- Pay me first
- Buffet paraphrases invest in business that is so wonderful an idiot can run them… because sooner or later one will.
- Fees kill wealth

- Think like a bank and earn like a bank
- The Money my money makes is taxed less than the money I make.
  - Take the emotion out of investing
    o By the time we hear something in the news the morning we wake up the market has already reacted, and we are already a day late and a dollar short
    - Track everything
    - No idle money
      o If I put $200 in my Roth or Passive income account, its invested right away
    - Cash diet
      o I learned my lesson after being balls-deep in debt.
- Read, read some more, and read it again 4 times

Fees kill wealth:

Years ago, a family member convinced to me buy two mutual funds GUT and GAB. GUT's expense ratio is 1.75% and GAB 1.37%. I was making a decent amount of dividends from them. I was happy as a clam. But then I educated myself and learned about expense ratios and how they can kill wealth. To say the least, when I found an online calculator and crunched my numbers, I shat my pantaloons! I was losing 1 quarter of dividends a year to the Expense ratio. I asked my family member how much he and his sister had in these two funds they were losing a substantial amount of $$$ to the expense ratio. His mentality was it's okay it's the price I pay for making a butt ton of money. My retort "but, wouldn't you want that $50k+ added to that total you were making??" Needless to say, it was a losing argument, and he wasn't going to budge. I got out of those two funds and put the cash into SPY (its in my traditional IRA) and VOO (in my Roth IRA). My returns weren't as big as with GUT and GAB, but I was losing less money to the Expense Ratio. In the long run I am doing better having swapped out.

If managers and brokers take *nothing* the investors receive everything (i.e. the total return of the stock market) (Bogle, 2017).

Invested	1% expense ratio per year
$1,000	$10
$10,000	$100
$100,000	$1,000

The rule of 72:

Rule of 72 Why is it useful? It is used to estimate the number of years required to double invested money at a given annual return.

Ticker	Yield	Rule 72	Years to double
T	5.91%	72/5.91	12.18
VOO	1.5%	72/1.5	50

I track my dividends to see how much I have made over the previous year.

Ex.

Date	Ticker	Div	Div subtotal	Div total
7/29/2022	NRZ	$2.82	$7.80	$405.14
08/01/2022	T	$24.53	$85.11	$429.67

Tracking this keeps me on schedule and shows me where I need to put my money to get to my first goal of $100 a year in dividends.

The World has its hair on fire!

It's mid-2022 and the news and a clamor with recession rumors, stock market crashes, and other Doom and gloom! I ignore it. I invest the same amount into the same companies that I have been investing in to generate more dividends so those dividends can make me more dividends. Currently, 2023 banks like JP Morgan and Bank of America are warning of impending doom and debt default. Will people panic now that these predictions of disaster are ringing?

I try to invest so that every month I have a dividend coming in.

Passive income

Passive income definition is a type of "unearned income" that is obtained automatically without much effort.

Dividends are a form of passive income now another chart

Ticker	$ per share	Div yield
JNJ	1.13	2.75%
HD	1.90	2.55%
T	0.28	6.58%
CRT	0.43	8.49%

How much to invest to get $1000/yr

T	$15,197
JNJ	$36,364
HD	$39,216
CRT	$11,779

Now a real-world example

I got $400 in birthday money, and I wanted to invest it rather than just spend it.

Ticker	*Invested*	*Shares*	*Dividend*
JNJ	$400.00	2.405	$2.72

I am going to earn approximately $11 a year off of this investment. I am only going to be putting the money I get for birthdays, Christmas, etc… into JNJ and just watching it grow. That same $400 put into a savings account would maybe get me $0.01. Win-win for me having invested in it.

The stock market is the greatest wealth-building tool on the planet as long as you know how to do basic math and understand the power of compounding.

The Me Tax:

We pay our bills, our car insurance, gym memberships and etc... but we seem to fail to pay ourselves. We should include "The Me Tax" in the list of things to pay. The Me Tax should go to our Roth IRAs, emergency accounts or passive income acco*unts*.

Everyone from The Richest Man in Babylon to Warren Buffet says to pay yourself first. Paying yourself first takes advantage of one of the best wealth producers Compound Interest.

What does this look like?

Paycheck: $1,650

10%- $165

15%- $248

20%- $330

If you put away this money how much would it be? I get paid bi-weekly so that means 24 paychecks

10%- $165- $3,960/ yr

15%- $248- $5,952/yr

20%- $330 - $7,920/ yr

Investing that money into the market in an index fund or a stock that pays a decent dividend will be the most intelligent thing to do. Savings accounts at big banks that pay .001% of your money will be losing value.

At the moment since interest rates have been on the rise with the ever-rising inflation level 2021-2022 and going; HYSA (high yield savings accounts) have seen their interest rates rise as well.

Now what?

So, you figured out what a dividend is, how to calculate how much to put away, etc… now what? What do I invest in? There are charts, books websites, influencers, etc all clamoring for my attention and money; how do I claw through this fog of war and make an intelligent decision?

Index funds are a low-cost way

Ticker	**DIVIDEND**
VOO	1.77%
SPY	1.73%
BND	2.68%

Investing in the S&P 500 index funds is a secure way to build wealth and take the difficulty out of buying individual stocks, you are buying an entire index of the top 500 companies.

Real-world example

Ticker	Holding	Latest Dividends Received	Total year to date (10/2022)
SPY	7.2013	$11.31	$32.74
VOO	12.2464	$17.91	$49.19

If you want to do individual securities best thing to do in my opinion is look around your house and look at where you shop. Looking into your cupboards or in your bathroom you can spot many companies in which to invest and collect dividends.

Ticker	DIVIDEND	DIVIDENDS PER SHARE	$ TO INVEST TO GET $100/YR
TGT	2.89%	$1.08	$3,460.20
KR	2.47%	$0.26	$4,048.58
JNJ	2.71%	$1.13	$3,690.03
PG	2.87%	$0.91	$3,484.32
UL	4.33%	$0.46	$2,309.47
CLX	3.60%	$1.18	$2,778
XOM	3.50%	$0.88	$2,857
CVX	3.52%	$1.42	$2,841

SHEL	3.89%	$0.50	$2,571
MCD	2.44%	$1.52	$4,098
SBUX	2.38%	$0.53	$4,202
COST	0.76%	$0.90	$13,157

Investing in what you routinely use is a good way to get paid for what you use. I shop at Target and Kroger stores often. My kids love McDonalds, and we eat and use products from Unilever and Procter and Gamble. For dang sure after the scamdemic Clorox became a household name and addiction right next to crack and Starbucks.

What's in your pocket?

Besides being buried in credit card debt Americans have things in their pocket they can invest in too. Once you pay off your credit card debt guess what that's a savings of 14.51%-19.20%. Instead of paying the credit card companies have them pay you with DIVIDENDS!

TICKER	DIVIDED YIELD	DIVIDEND PER SHARE	$ INVESTED FOR $100/YR
V	0.80%	$0.38	$12,500
MA	0.65%	$0.49	$15,385

| DFS | 2.49% | $0.60 | $4,016 |
| AXP | 1.42% | $0.52 | $7,043 |

Doesn't it sound better that credit card companies pay you instead of you paying them?

Crypto:

I stayed clear of the crypto craze; I tend to be suspicious of things that are "the next hot thing." Crypto is worth only what the next guy is willing to pay. The entire cryptocurrency market is small relative to other asset markets as to world economic activity. The way it captured the imagination of the public, as well as the spillover effects into other markets, were eerily similar to the madness that accompanied the dot.com bubble (Malkiel, 2020). It is the extreme volatility in the value of bitcoin that makes it fail the common definition of money. An asset that gains and loses a substantial percentage of its initial value each day will serve neither as a useful unit of account nor as a dependable store of value. There is no natural anchor for the value of a cryptocurrency (Malkiel, 2020).

Who do you trust with your money?

Who do I trust with my money? A broker? A money manager? Or some influencer who says they have the magic formula? None of the above. I trust myself above all because I care about my money more than these fee-charging leeches. As I mentioned before fees kill wealth faster than anything.

Many influencers or brokers will brag about how they beat the market or have a magic formula to turn your $1,000 into $1 million. They claim to 10x your money and make you rich beyond your imagination. The truth is these people are normally right once in maybe a hundred times and are wrong more often. These managers and brokers often charge huge fees that will wipe out most of your gains. Their main goal is to make money and to use your money to do it. Their portfolios have tonnes of movement because they are actively managed. One whiff of bad news on the net or airwaves and they start making moves.

What can you do? For one ignore the static, research, and don't panic. When the market drops see it as an opportunity. The market is on sale and the prices are at their true value and not at their inflated values. You're able to purchase more shares are a lower price and all your dividends purchase more at a premium. Buy and hold, ride out the dip.

Proselytizing

The definition of the word proselytizing is "the act of attempting to convert someone from one religion, belief, or opinion to another."

I can try to proselytize all day to try to convince you to invest one way or another but its literally up to you. God gave us free will and in that, we chose to do what benefits us. You can choose to follow the crowd who wants instant gratification and blows their money on coke, whores, and fancy cars or you can invest. People complain all the time that they never came from money or generational wealth like all the other rich people. Generational wealth has to start from somewhere I chose for it to start with me.

I chose not to join the choir of wasted talent and decided to start investing not only for me but for generations after me.

Investing is a skill not taught in schools, how to make money, make money and become wealthy. Instead, young children are influenced by rappers and rockstars with gold chains and cars. Being wealthy also means learning how to keep the money you earn and not burn it on useless things.

Investing intelligence comes with time and trial. Research needs to be done and patience exercised. Habits need to be honed and lessons and wisdom passed down.

Beware of get-rich schemes, pyramid schemes, and other scams out there listen to the silence instead of the clamor. The chorus of people trying to ram influence down your throat. Learn to look past it and avoid the consequence of being foolhardy.

www.ingramcontent.com/pod-product-compliance
Lightning Source LLC
Chambersburg PA
CBHW050329220526
45465CB00005B/2205